A Very Young Skater

Also by Jill Krementz

The Face of South Vietnam
(with text by Dean Brelis)

*Sweet Pea—A Black Girl
Growing Up in the Rural South*

Words and Their Masters
(with text by Israel Shenker)

A Very Young Dancer

A Very Young Rider

A Very Young Gymnast

A Very Young Circus Flyer

A Very Young Skater

Written and Photographed by

Jill Krementz

Alfred A. Knopf, New York, 1979

This is a Borzoi Book
published by Alfred A. Knopf, Inc.
Copyright © 1979 by Jill Krementz
All rights reserved under International and Pan-American Copyright Conventions.
Published in the United States by Alfred A. Knopf, Inc., New York, and
simultaneously in Canada by Random House of Canada Limited, Toronto.
Distributed by Random House, Inc., New York.

Library of Congress Cataloging in Publication Data
Krementz, Jill
A very young skater.
1. Skating—Juvenile literature.
2. Healy, Katherine—Juvenile literature.
3. Skaters—Biography—Juvenile literature.
[1. Ice skating.   2. Ice skaters]
I. Title.
GV849.K73   796.9′1   79-2209
ISBN 0-394-50833-5

Manufactured in the United States of America
First Edition

This book has been sanctioned by the United States Figure Skating Association.

This book is dedicated, with much love,
to my sister, Christie Graham —
and to her daughter, Paget Graham,
who is also a very young skater.

—J.K.

My name is Katherine Healy, and I've been skating since I was three. I'm ten now. I do both figure skating and free skating. Figure skaters have to pass eight tests in order to qualify for the Olympic or World Level competitions. I'm hoping to pass my second test this year.

I really love performing, and I'm hoping that when I grow up I might be able to have my own ice show like John Curry. I like his style of skating the best. It's like ballet on ice.

I started skating because my parents loved to go skating. They used to take me to the rink because it was easier than getting a baby-sitter. We still have fun skating together. I love it when we go to Rockefeller Center on Saturday mornings.

Rockefeller Center is so pretty, especially when the Christmas tree is all lit up. Last year they had a tree-lighting ceremony, and I did a special exhibition.

I go to St. Ann's Episcopal School in Brooklyn Heights, where I live. I take five academic subjects—science, math, English, history, and Latin. Latin is my favorite.

My schedule is arranged so I can leave early and have plenty of time for skating. I don't have to take gym because I get so much exercise on my own. During the week I skate every day for two or three hours and then I have a ballet class.

I usually go home around noon for a quick lunch, and then we get ready to go to the rink.

I skate at Sky Rink, which is the largest indoor rink in New York City. As soon as we get inside, I sign up for a patch of ice so I can practice my figures. It's called patching, and a session lasts for forty-five minutes.

They have a special barre in the lounge, and I like to warm up for about ten minutes before I go out on the ice.

Then I go into the ladies locker room and put on my skates. Lacing takes a lot of practice because it has to be done exactly right. I pull the laces very tight up to my instep, and then I loosen them up a bit so I can bend forward a little. It's important to tuck in your lace ends so you don't trip over them.

Figure skating means you have to be able to execute different kinds of figures on the ice with the blade of your skate. There are forty-two different figures, but it takes years of practice to be able to do them all. I can do ten.

All forty-two figures are based on circles—you just do them on different edges of your blade and in different directions. The diameter of your circle is supposed to be three times your body length. When you're being tested, you have to be able to lay out your figures without any help, but when you're learning or just practicing, it helps to lay them out with a scribe.

A scribe is what you use to trace a circle on the ice—it's a big compass with a point on one end of it. Scribing is also a good way to check your circles if you've laid them out on your own.

No matter which figure I'm doing, I always push off from what's called the center
— that's where two circles meet. Sometimes, when I forget, I push off with my
toe pick, but I really shouldn't do that because it makes my center messy and the
judges don't like that. It's best if you push off with the edge of your free foot.

I skate on either the inside or the outside edge of my blade, depending on which
figure I'm working on. You have to be able to feel the edges with your foot. Flat-
ting your edges is bad—that's when both edges of your blade are on the ice at the
same time. Lots of skaters don't even wear socks so they can feel their edges better.

You have to stay on the same foot throughout the first circle, without putting your free foot down. Then, when you get back to the center and move onto the second circle, you usually switch feet—except on serpentine figures, where you stay on the same foot but change your edge.

I always wear a sweater, mittens, and leg warmers because it's easier to concentrate if you're not freezing to death.

My coach's name is Glyn Watts, and he's from England. He skated in the World's and the Olympics in Ice Dancing, and he and his partner, Hilary Green, were Britain's National Champions for five years. Ice Dancing is when you skate set patterns on the ice with a partner. You don't have any lifts or throws. When you have them it's called Pairs, which is another category. Glyn also used to be a champion roller skater.

I have lessons with him three times a week.

Body position is very important in figure skating. You should look about three feet in front of where you're going. You can't drop your head too much when you look down because if you do it throws off your body balance.

Glyn practically has to mold my body into the right position to make me feel how I should stand to skate a perfect circle. It's hard enough to draw a perfect circle with a pencil, much less with your foot.

Sometimes Glyn skates along behind to correct me if I'm doing something wrong, but usually he just watches so he can keep an eye on my tracings.

My biggest problem in figures is pressing into the ice and making a good firm tracing. I tend to wobble a little too much, so my tracings have wiggles in them.

My tracings are often so light we have to lie down on the ice to see them.

Glyn says he's going to put weights on my ankles so he won't have to get his tummy so cold.

Even people like John Curry spend a lot of time practicing their school figures. Of course his figures are a lot more complicated than mine. When he won the Olympic gold medal for Great Britain in 1976, his figures got especially high scores.

At the end of a session we usually patch up any holes made by our toe picks, and then they resurface the ice for a free-skate session. They use a big truck called a Zamboni, named after a famous skater. It has blades on the bottom to scrape the ice, and then it lays down a sheet of water for a smooth finish.

While they're resurfacing, I like to go to the snack bar with my friend Dale for hot chocolate and a bagel with cream cheese. Dale's mother skates in ice shows.

Then I change into my free skates. They're almost like my patch skates except there's an extra point on the toe pick that makes it easier to dig into the ice when you're going for a jump.

Before putting patch skates away, it's very important to clean any slush off the blades and to cover them with terry cloth booties so they won't rust.

A free-skate session usually lasts for an hour, and that's when I work on my jumps and spins and other footwork. I like to warm up a little beforehand so my body will be nice and flexible. Then I stroke around the ice for a while, which means I just skate around the rink very fast.

Free skating means skating to music, and we all take turns playing our own. I like classical music the best, but lots of the other skaters prefer rock or disco.

When I work on my spirals, Glyn reminds me to keep my bottom down and my hips pressed forward.

On a spiral, your free foot and your head should be on the same level and your back should be nicely arched.

I like to wait until I'm good and limber before working on my jumps. The hardest part is concentrating on the angle of my feet.

I love doing split jumps because it's like flying. It makes me feel free, like a bird. When I take off my sweater it makes me feel even lighter. Birds are luckier though, because they don't have to worry about pointing their feet.

I also work on spread eagles and sit spins…which are sometimes just plain sit *downs* instead. If you do fall, and every skater falls millions of times, the most important thing is to just relax and go with the fall—and to get your hands off the ice as soon as possible so another skater won't run over your fingers.

I'm a member of the Junior Skating Club of New York, and every Friday afternoon we have a skating session just for fun. Miss Peppe is in charge, and she used to be a famous skater. She invented the layback spin and made our Olympic team three times. She and Sonja Henie were friends.

Linda Catanzaro is my best friend, and we like to shadow dance together. That's when you skate side by side doing the same patterns. Patrick Greenaway is another good friend. This year he won the disco competition at Flushing Meadow Park.

Kyoko Ina is only six, and already performing in exhibitions. We have the best time doing wheelbarrows. She's usually the wheelbarrow since she's so little.

We play lots of games, especially on holidays, and Glyn tries not to get trampled by us.

At the end of each session, we always line up in pairs for a grand march around the rink. Miss Peppe plays special march music and tells us to look smart and keep the line straight, but somehow we never quite manage.

At Christmas time we have a special pageant and everyone gets all dressed up. Last Christmas the three chairwomen of the club were cowboy ladies and the boys were Santa's elves.

The rest of us were reindeer and snowflakes.

We also have competitions, and last year I did a dance to the music of the ballet *Don Quixote*. I ended by kneeling on the ice and throwing back my head.

When they gave out the prizes, I won two trophies—one to keep, and a fancier one that belongs to the club and which I only get to keep for a year, until the next competition. But my name gets engraved on that one.

Ballet lessons are a very important part of my training, and I take dance class every day after skating. Twice a week I study with Madame Nemchinova. She is from Russia, and she used to be a famous dancer with Diaghilev's Ballets Russes.

When I arrive she gives me a kiss.

Madame always tells me that I have two arms, two legs, and one head and that she wants me to use *every*thing.

While I'm dancing she keeps saying, "Happy Face...Happy Face!"

At the end of my lesson she gives me a lollipop. She says it's good for the throat.

Three times a week I have classes at George Balanchine's School of American Ballet.

My teacher's name is Miss Reiman, and she always tells me that ballet is wonderful for my skating but she's not sure it works the other way around.

I've been in quite a few ballets because Mr. Balanchine uses so many children in his productions for the New York City Ballet. Last year I got picked to play Marie in *The Nutcracker,* which meant a lot of rehearsals with David Richardson and with Mr. B. himself.

I had to cut down on my skating schedule in order to have time for all my performances. Peter Boal danced the part of the Prince.

My ballet classes are usually over by six, and so Mommy and I pick up Daddy at his office—he's a lawyer—and we all drive home together.

After dinner, I do my homework and then I go to bed around nine-thirty or ten. Daddy calls me "one-more-page-Katherine" because I like to read before I go to sleep. I'd read all night if I could get away with it.

Saturdays are when we catch up on a lot of errands—like if I need new skates.

I get my skating boots from Mr. Klingbeil on Long Island. He's been making boots for about thirty years.

First he measures my feet by tracing them in a book, and he also takes a lot of other measurements. Then he makes a pair of wooden models of my feet, and they are called the lasts. After that, using the wooden forms, he makes a pattern out of paper—like a dressmaking pattern. He uses that to cut the leather for the boot, and then he stitches it all together.

When you try on boots, it's important to bend your legs without lifting your heels so you don't break the soles. That's because the boot has been designed to go on a blade.

After the boots are ready, we take them to the shop at Sky Rink to get the blades put on. Most skaters like to have their blades mounted near an ice rink so that they can test them out right away and be sure they're properly positioned. The blades are made of stainless steel. The first skates ever were invented in northern Europe. The skaters used to tie strips of bones under their feet and push themselves along the ice with long poles—like skiers. Then, around the fifteenth century, the Dutch invented the first bladed skates and when the canals froze, they skated all the time. That's how they got to school or the market. They even skated to church.

It takes about a week to break in a new pair of boots. When boots don't fit properly, you can get bone spurs on your feet—and that hurts!

Mommy makes all my skating costumes, so sometimes we go down to Orchard Street, where they have lots of pretty fabrics.

Another place I love to visit is Cinderella Flowers. It's fun to rummage through all the odd boxes. They have over two thousand different kinds of fake flowers.

When Mommy pins a new costume, she always tells me not to wriggle.

Saturday night is when we usually go to the ballet. Gelsey Kirkland is my very favorite ballerina. Whenever she dances, I go backstage to her dressing room after the performance and say hello. I met her when I was five, and we've been friends ever since.

She always gives me a few flowers from her bouquet, and I put them in my hair.

Saturday nights are also when our skating club puts on exhibitions. This year Glyn and his wife, Christine, showed us their special dance program, which they had just performed in Spain, where they won the World Professional Championships.

Sometimes I perform—and what's really exciting, so does John Curry when he's in New York.

On Sundays, Mommy, Daddy, and I sleep very late and spend the rest of the day relaxing. I like to work on my stamp collection and play with my dolls.

My room has a barre in it so I can practice ballet. Daddy built it all by himself.

The other thing I do on weekends—but only two or three times a year—is go to competitions. I only compete in nonqualifying free-skating meets because I haven't passed my second test yet. It's good experience though, because it gets you used to performing in front of a lot of people. When I compete, I'm representing the Skating Club of New York.

When you arrive, you register and hand in your music at a special table.

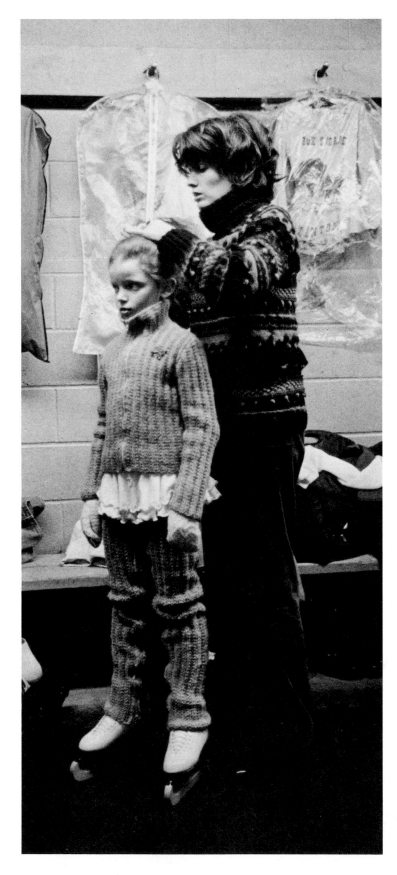

They have a locker room for competitors, and each group has its own warm-up session for about twenty minutes. The real trick is *staying* warm until it's your turn to compete.

Glyn usually comes along, and he tells me to think about what I'm doing and to stay calm and not get nervous. Sometimes I think he's the one who's nervous. For me, it's just fun.

They give you an order to skate in, and I'm happiest when I get to go in the middle. I don't like to be first because the ice is too wet and slippery, and towards the end it's all chopped up.

A free-style program is supposed to last two minutes, but it can be ten seconds shorter or longer. The judges aren't supposed to judge anything after the timer blows his whistle.

The judges post the scores for each category on a special bulletin board. Then they award the prizes at the end of the day.

Last year Julie Wasserman, Ricky Coleman, and I all won trophies in the Girls Pre-Juvenile Singles Competition.

One way I learn a lot is by watching others, especially John Curry, who is my idol. This year he starred in his own ice show on Broadway, called *Ice Dancing*.

He did a wonderful number called *Tango Jalousie*, which starts off with a solo.

Then he and JoJo Starbuck, the co-star of his show, did a very dramatic pas de deux.

I also liked it when he skated Debussy's *Afternoon of a Faun* with Cathy Foulkes.

This past summer John taught a special class at Sky Rink. One of the reasons he decided to teach is because he wants to help other people skate from an artistic rather than a competitive point of view.

We had lessons twice a week, on Mondays and Fridays. We started each session with warm-ups. First we did exercises at the barre to warm our feet and bodies, and then we worked on port de bras, which means arm movements. John kept reminding us to be conscious of our hands, the way dancers are.

One day he taught us a special routine with movements like a Russian folk dance.

He made us practice stroking around the rink with our hands on our hips because that's a good way to learn to keep your tummy in.

Most of the time he worked with us as a group, but sometimes he worked with each of us individually.

I also took ballet with David Howard as part of John's summer program. There are mostly grown-ups in his classes.

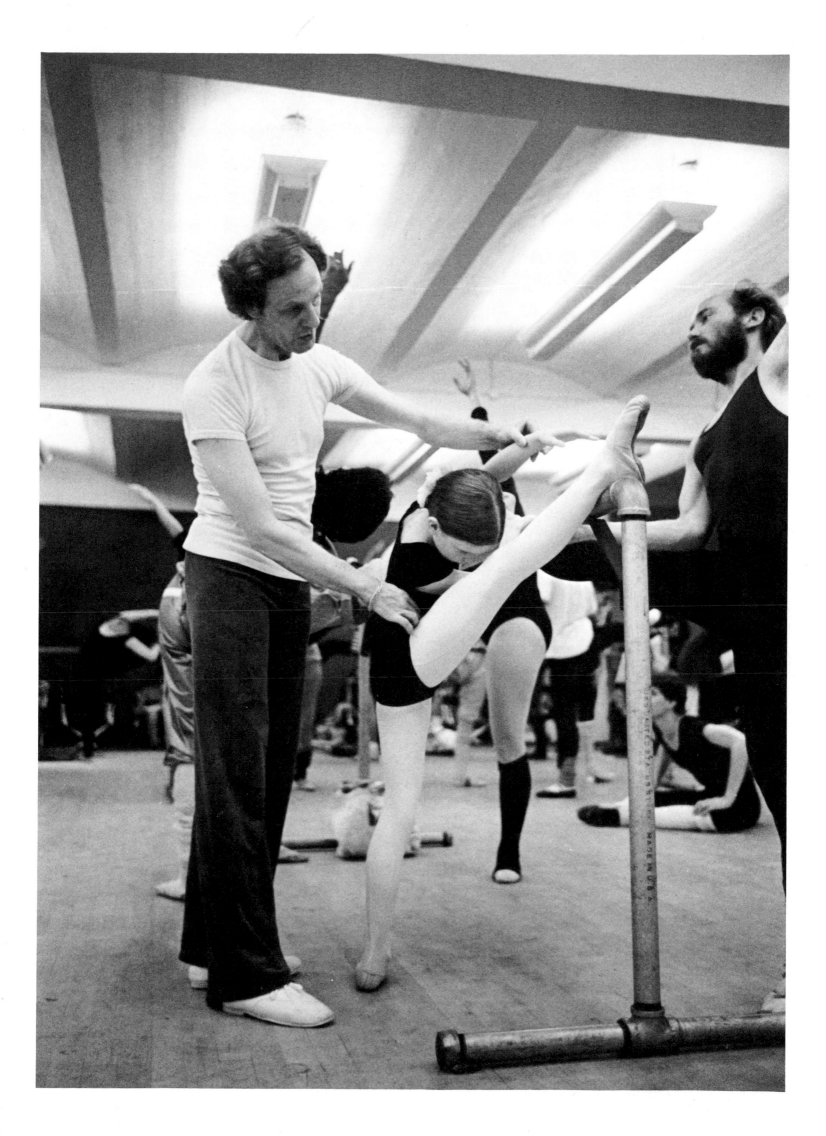

At the end of the summer, a very exciting thing happened. I was invited to be in Superskates—a big skating show held once a year at Madison Square Garden. Lots of the best skaters perform, and the money goes to the United States Olympic Fund.

John gave Mommy a sketch for what I should wear. He told her to make it with several layers of pastel-colored chiffon so it would look more like a ballet costume and not the usual skating dress.

Getting my music ready was the next important step. John and I decided on two segments from Offenbach's *Le Papillon*, which means "The Butterfly." I took a phonograph record to an audio engineer named John Snell in order to have it transferred to tape. I got to hold the stopwatch while we were timing it.

Then John and I worked on a special program that he choreographed for me.

We rented ice in the middle of the night to work out my patterns.

We had two days of rehearsals with Harry Woolever, who's the director of Super-skates.

They taped the rehearsal schedules on our dressing room doors.

On the first day, we mostly practiced the big production numbers, especially the Finale, where we all had to carry big flags. Sonya Dunfield showed me a special way to hold the flag so it wouldn't get the better of me. Sonya used to be our National Champion, and after that she was a big star in Holiday on Ice.

The flag was really heavy, and the pole kept hitting my nose.

While we were rehearsing, the production staff worked backstage making special screens for our entrances and exits.

On the day of the performance, John came over to see how I was doing and to wish me luck.

We did a technical run-through and tested the lights.

All of the performers were given rooms at a hotel across from Madison Square Garden, so that's where we went after the rehearsal was over. While I took a nap, Daddy polished my skates.

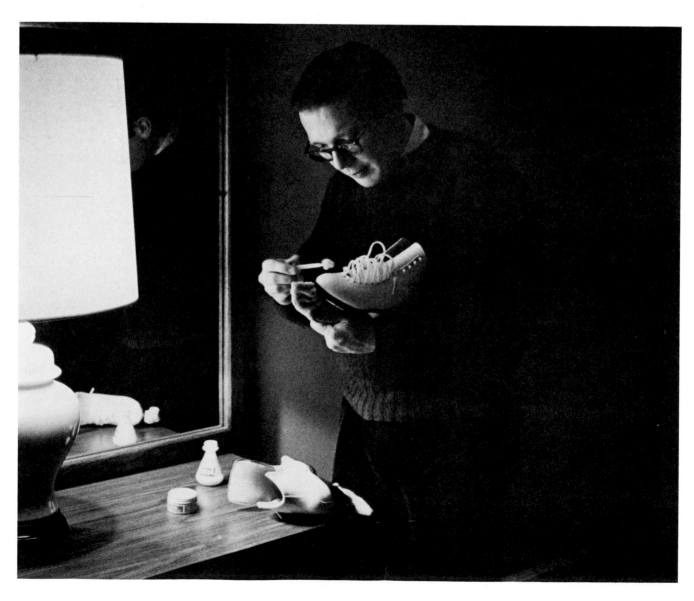

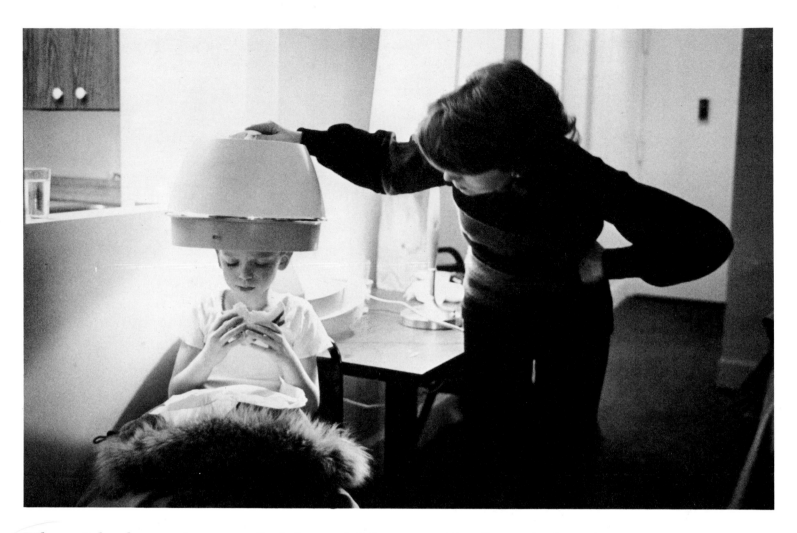

Then I had a turkey sandwich and Mommy fixed my hair. She put a little rouge on my cheeks so the spotlights wouldn't make me look too white.

Around seven o'clock we walked over to the Garden. John and Glyn both sent me beautiful bouquets of flowers.

Daddy wasn't allowed to stay in the ladies dressing room, so he just gave me a good luck kiss and went out to sit with the audience.

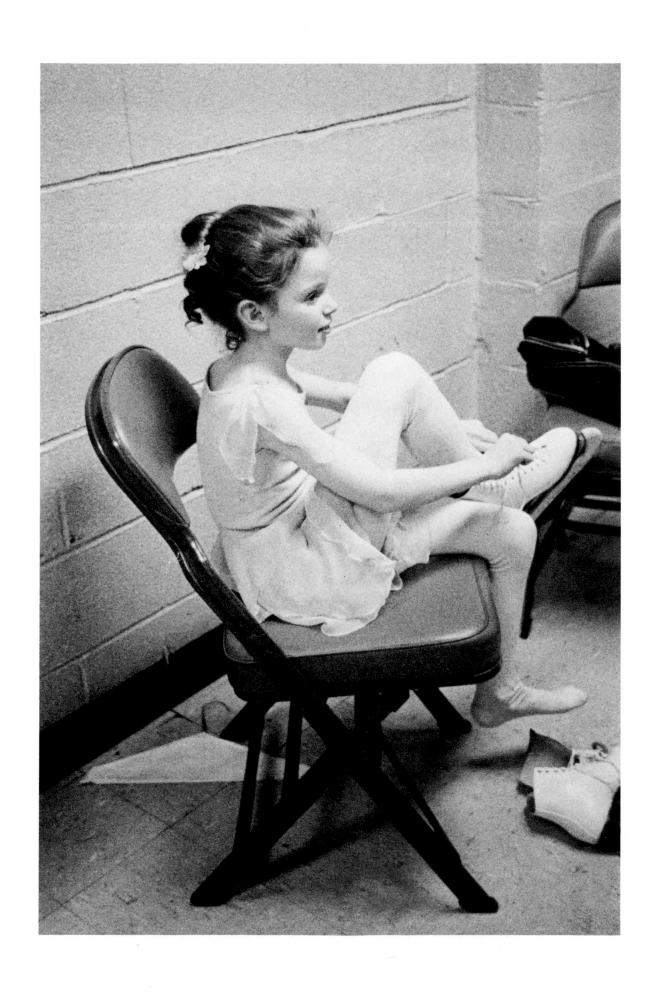

Soon it was time to start getting ready.

The show began. Toller Cranston is one of my favorite skaters. He's from Canada, and he skates at our rink whenever he's in New York. He always wears black.

Linda Fratianne didn't start skating until she was nine. But she made up for lost time because she became the United States National Champion when she was sixteen and went on to win the World's.

Charlie Tickner is our National Men's Champion, and he's famous for his high clean jumps. He used to be very nervous, and so he learned how to hypnotize himself in order to relax.

Lisa-Marie Allen is another beautiful skater. She's also a very good horseback rider.

JoJo Starbuck and Ken Shelley used to be our Pairs Champions before they turned professional. They met when they were nine years old and they were both snow-flakes in a skating recital called *Winter Wonderland*.

They did an inside spread eagle together, which is really hard.

Tai Babilonia and Randy Gardner have been United States Pairs Champions since 1976, and in 1979 they became World Champions. They throw each other all over the place.

My program lasted two minutes and forty seconds. I could hear people clapping, but mostly I was concentrating on the music and what I was doing.

I knew John and Glyn were both watching, so I wanted to do well.

I ended my program with four curtsies—one to each side of the Garden.

Afterwards, Madame Nemchinova came backstage to say hello. She had never seen me skate before.

John gave me a big kiss and said how proud he was of me.

After Superskates was over, two more exciting things happened to me. The first was I got to start dancing on toe!

It's very important to put on toe shoes exactly right, because if there's a bump in the lambswool stuffing it's very painful.

At first I started with five minutes or so at the barre, after my regular lesson, but now I can do a little in the center. Not much though.

And the other good thing that happened was that I passed my second test, which means I can compete in North Atlantics if I want to.

But even though I passed, the judges all commented that my tracings were still too light and that my circles were too large. And they said I was wobbling too much.

It's going to be a very busy year. Skating is so much fun, but getting rid of the wobbles won't be all that easy!

A Note About the Author

Jill Krementz is a well-known photographer of literary figures, a documentary photographer, and an author. Her pictures can be seen regularly in *The New York Times, New York* magazine, *People, Newsweek,* and other major periodicals, and she has photographs in the permanent collection of the Museum of Modern Art. Her previous books include *Sweet Pea, A Very Young Dancer, A Very Young Rider, A Very Young Gymnast,* and *A Very Young Circus Flyer.* Recently she was chosen to take the official portraits of four members of the United States Cabinet.

A Note on the Type

This book was set in a film version of Bulmer, a distinguished type-face long famous in the history of English printing, which was de-signed and cut by William Martin in about 1790 for William Bulmer of the Shakespeare Press. In design, it is all but a modern face, with vertical stress, sharp differentiation between the thick and thin strokes, and nearly flat serifs. The italic is taken from a font of Baskerville; Martin was John Baskerville's pupil.

The text was composed by Quad Typographers, Inc., New York, New York. The book was printed by Halliday Lithographers, West Hanover, Massachusetts, and bound by American Book–Stratford Press, Saddle Brook, New Jersey.

Graphics were directed by R. D. Scudellari; book design and layout by Virginia Tan, based on designs by Elissa Ichiyasu.